Contents

HSEBOOKS

The **health and safety** *system in Great Britain*

© *Crown copyright 2002*

Applications for reproduction should be made in writing to:
Copyright Unit, Her Majesty's Stationery Office, St Clements House,
2-16 Colegate, Norwich NR3 1BQ

First published 1992
Second edition 1998
Third edition 2002

ISBN 0 7176 2243 6

Foreword

This guide outlines the occupational health and safety system in Great Britain. It responds to the many requests for information we receive from international visitors, inquirers and researchers, although many in Great Britain will also find it informative.

This new edition is available for the first time on HSE's worldwide website – an efficient way of reaching a global audience. Occupational health and safety is increasingly a subject for international debate – whether via policy or legislative developments in the European Union, the collection and dissemination of information and good practice by the European Agency, or the work and programmes of other international bodies such as the International Labour Organisation, the Organisation for Economic Co-operation and Development, and the World Health Organisation. The Health and Safety Commission and Executive (HSC/E) seeks to engage in these processes and aims to play an active role in the development of international occupational health and safety thinking and practice.

Each country will have its own health and safety priorities, traditions and institutions – so there is no one set of solutions valid for all times and circumstances. However, engagement in the debate, and the fostering of bilateral contacts with our counterparts in other countries are mutually beneficial; we share similar problems, we should share information and good practice.

This guide describes a health and safety structure which is integrated (across industry sectors), based on tripartism (the co-operation of Government and the social partners), and societal involvement (via consultation and engagement), and is aimed at delivering a proportionate, targeted and risk-based approach.

Bill Callaghan
Chair Health and Safety Commission

Key facts

1 . . . . . . Almost all the risks to health and safety arising from work activity in Britain are regulated through a single legal framework. The regulatory concerns of the Health and Safety Commission (HSC) and the Health and Safety Executive (HSE) range from health and safety in nuclear installations and mines, through to factories, farms, hospitals and schools, offshore gas and oil installations, the safety of the gas grid and the movement of dangerous goods and substances, railway safety, and many other aspects of the protection both of workers and the public. In addition, over 400 local authorities are responsible for enforcement in a wide range of other activities, including the retail and finance sectors, and other parts of the services sector, particularly leisure.

2 . . . . . . HSC and HSE are non-departmental bodies with specific statutory functions in relation to health and safety. The Commission is appointed by the Secretary of State for Transport, Local Government and the Regions who, in turn, appoint the Executive. The Executive employs around 4000 staff including policy advisers, inspectors, technologists and scientific and medical advisers. The functions of HSC and HSE are performed on behalf of the crown, their staff are civil servants.

3 . . . . . . The Commission's statutory responsibilities under the Health and Safety at Work etc Act 1974 (HSW Act)[1] include proposing health and safety law and standards to Ministers. In preparing its proposals, the Commission relies on the advice of the Executive and on scientific research carried out in the Executive's laboratories and through out-house programmes. It also consults extensively with a wide variety of organisations representing professional interests in health and safety, business managers, trades unions, scientific and technological experts. This is managed through a network of advisory committees and by public invitation to comment on particular proposals. Special efforts are made to seek the views of small firms, often using a wide range of intermediary organisations, often representing trade, sector, or business interests.

4 . . . . . . The standards of health and safety achieved in Great Britain are delivered by the flexible regulatory system introduced in 1974 by the HSW Act, and are typified by the Management of Health and Safety at Work Regulations

1999 (MHSWR).[2] They also reflect a long tradition of health and safety regulation going back to the 19th century. Since the HSW Act was passed, HSC has been engaged in progressive reform of the law, seeking to replace detailed industry-specific legislation with a modern approach in which regulations, wherever possible, express goals and general principles and detailed requirements are placed in codes and guidance. Approved codes have a special place in British health and safety law – they set out ways of achieving standards. Those who depart from the code must be prepared to show that their own approach is an equally valid way of meeting the legal requirements. In this way, flexibility is allowed for technological development, within a framework set by mandatory regulations.

5 . . . . . . A fundamental principle of the British system is that responsibility for health and safety lies with those who own, manage and work in industrial and commercial undertakings. This includes the self-employed. They must assess the risks attached to their activity and take appropriate action. Workforce involvement and in particular the work of safety representatives has made an important contribution to raising standards of health and safety in the last 25 years.

6 . . . . . . The need to reduce risks and take appropriate action lies behind the qualification 'so far as is reasonably practicable', which is widely used in British health and safety law. This, in effect, requires that good practice should be followed whenever it is established, and sets the high standard that is 'reasonably practicable' for the duty holder to take precautions up to the point where the taking of further measures would be grossly disproportionate to any residual risk.

7 . . . . . . In enforcing the law, health and safety inspectors have important statutory powers. They can and do enter premises without warning. If they are not satisfied by health and safety standards they can issue improvement notices requiring problems to be put right within a specified time, serve a prohibition notice either with immediate effect or deferred, or prosecute for the most serious failings.

8 . . . . . . Some health and safety inspectors are trained in systems and principles applicable to a wide range of activities, while others specialise in a single

high-risk industry, for example, nuclear, mining, railways or offshore oil. All are highly trained to use discretion in applying the law and to feed information back to the policy and technical centres of HSE. All can call, where necessary, on the experience and expertise within their own and other inspectorates and elsewhere in HSE.

The system

▼ ## The Health and Safety at Work etc Act 1974[1]

9 . . . . . . Great Britain has a tradition of health and safety regulation going back over 150 years. The present system came into being in 1974 when the HSW Act set up new institutions and provided for the progressive revision and replacement of all health and safety law then existing.

The main institutions

10 . . . . . . Two new institutions were created by the Act:

 Health and Safety Commission – a body of up to ten people, appointed by the Secretary of State for Transport, Local Government and the Regions after consultation with organisations representing employers, employees, local authorities and others, as appropriate. One of the present members of the Commission has been appointed to represent the public interest. HSC's primary function is to make arrangements to secure the health, safety and welfare of people at work, and the public, in the way undertakings are conducted; including proposing new law and standards, conducting research, providing information and advice, and controlling explosives and other dangerous substances. It has a specific duty to maintain the Employment Medical Advisory Service (EMAS), which provides advice on occupational health matters. It also has a general duty to help and encourage people concerned with all these matters.

 Health and Safety Executive – a body of three people appointed by the Commission with the consent of the Secretary of State for Transport, Local Government and the Regions. The Executive advises and assists the Commission in its functions. It has some specific statutory responsibilities of its own, notably for the enforcement of health and safety law. The Executive's staff, approximately 4000, include inspectors, policy advisers, technologists and scientific and medical experts – collectively known as HSE.

11 . . . . . . The HSW Act and related legislation, is enforced by HSE, or by local authorities, according to the main activity carried out at individual work premises. The Health and Safety (Enforcing Authority) Regulations 1998

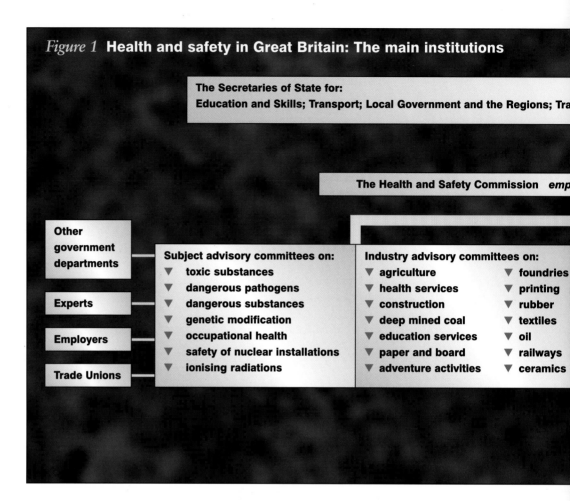

Figure 1 Health and safety in Great Britain: The main institutions

The Secretaries of State for:
Education and Skills; Transport; Local Government and the Regions; Tra

The Health and Safety Commission emp

Other government departments

Experts

Employers

Trade Unions

Subject advisory committees on:
▼ toxic substances
▼ dangerous pathogens
▼ dangerous substances
▼ genetic modification
▼ occupational health
▼ safety of nuclear installations
▼ ionising radiations

Industry advisory committees on:
▼ agriculture
▼ health services
▼ construction
▼ deep mined coal
▼ education services
▼ paper and board
▼ adventure activities

▼ foundries
▼ printing
▼ rubber
▼ textiles
▼ oil
▼ railways
▼ ceramics

(EA Regulations)[3] allocate the enforcement of health and safety legislation at different premises between local authorities and HSE.

12 . . . . . . **Local authorities** also have statutory responsibilities for enforcement of health and safety law in certain premises. These are mainly in the distribution, retail, office, leisure and catering sectors. HSE liaises closely with local authorities on enforcement matters through the Health and Safety Executive/Local Authorities Enforcement Liaison Committee (HELA). An enforcement liaison officer network in HSE regional offices across Britain also provides advice and support for local authorities.

Ministerial responsibilities

13 . . . . . . Health and safety is regulated in the same way across the whole of Great Britain and a number of different Secretaries of State are responsible to Parliament at Westminster for the activities of HSC and HSE in different areas. The Secretary of State for Transport, Local Government and the

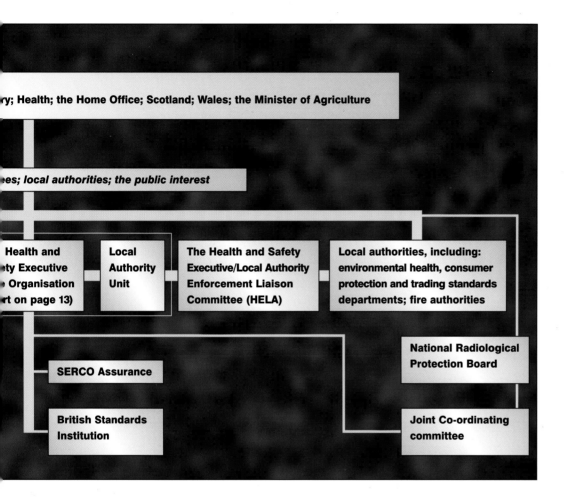

ry; Health; the Home Office; Scotland; Wales; the Minister of Agriculture

es; *local authorities; the public interest*

Regions answers to Parliament on HSC and HSE's staffing and resourcing,
on matters affecting protection of workers and on all other activities of the
Commission and Executive, except when these come within the specific
area of responsibility of another Secretary of State, ie, Trade and Industry on
nuclear safety and health and safety aspects of barriers to trade, and the
Ministry of Agriculture, on certain aspects of pesticide safety. In most of
these matters, the Commission, Executive and local authorities act by virtue
of their powers and duties under the HSW Act and its associated legislation,
or European legislation. In a few, they act under agreements as the agent of
the Secretary of State concerned.

14 . . . . . . Secretaries of State have the power to direct the Commission in particular
matters and they themselves may introduce health and safety law, provided
that they consult the Commission. In practice, almost all health and safety
proposals since the 1974 Act have been put forward to Ministers by the
Commission. In exercising their responsibilities for negotiating and

implementing European health and safety law, Ministers have always looked to the Commission for help and advice.

Advisory committees

15 . . . . . . HSE provides the Commission with policy, technological and professional advice. Other expert advice comes from HSC's network of advisory committees who deal with particular hazard areas and some with particular industries. Each includes a balance of employer and employee representatives and, where appropriate, technological and professional experts. The committees are supported by HSE, whose main function is to recommend standards and guidance and, in some cases, to comment on policy issues confronting HSC or to recommend an approach to a particular new problem.

Consultation

16 . . . . . . HSE consults informally on the Commission's behalf with those who are likely to be affected by any proposal before it goes forward to the formal stage. Though this process frequently makes use of the advisory committee network, it normally extends more widely. Within HSE, policy staff tap the expertise of inspectors, scientists and technologists during the process of working up proposals into a practical form. Local authorities are also consulted through the HSE/Local Authority Enforcement Liaison Committee (HELA).

17 . . . . . . Before it puts forward proposals for new legislation or codes of practice to Ministers, HSC issues formal consultation documents which are made publicly available and which have a very wide circulation. This ensures that HSC, in finalising its proposals, is aware of the views of a wide range of people and institutions who may be affected by new health and safety provisions.

18 . . . . . . The same procedure is followed whether the proposed law on standards originated domestically or from the European Union (EU). Though the consultation process in the latter case is necessarily constrained by the terms of the legislation, questions will normally arise about application and interpretation, about the chosen method of implementing the directive, and about any options or consequences for the reform of related UK law. In

every case it is HSC's objective to ensure, both in the negotiation of European proposals and in their implementation, that established UK standards are maintained or improved.

19 . . . . . . The Commission and Executive have links with other bodies, notably universities, engineering institutions and the National Radiological Protection Board, which has a national function in relation to ionising and other radiations. Close contact is also maintained with professional and scientific societies, for example, the Royal Society, the British Occupational Hygiene Society, the Institute of Occupational Hygienists and the Royal Society of Chemistry, which make a major input into the development of the scientific and technical base of occupational health and safety in the UK.

20 . . . . . . Internationally, HSC and HSE assist and co-operate with the main institutions – notably those of the European Union (the Directorates General of the Commission, their advisory committees and working groups, the European Agency for Safety and Health at Work), but also those of the Organisation for Economic Co-operation and Development (OECD), the International Labour Office (ILO), the World Health Organisation (WHO), and the International Atomic Energy Agency (IAEA) in developing and applying international standards, codes and guides.

Limits of the Commission's responsibilities

21 . . . . . . Certain areas of risk or harm, directly or indirectly related to work activity, are covered by legislation other than the HSW Act and are not dealt with by HSC. These include consumer and food safety, marine and aviation safety and pollution.

The Health and Safety Executive

Organisation

22 . . . . . . The Health and Safety Executive brings together staff from a range of different backgrounds including:

- ▼ administrators and lawyers with experience of policy development in government departments;
- ▼ inspectors;
- ▼ scientists, technologists and medical professionals;
- ▼ information and communications specialists, statisticians and economists;
- ▼ finance, accounts and personnel specialists.

Policy

23 . . . . . . Policy staff from all these backgrounds, but predominantly career adminis-trators, work together in HSE's strategy, policy and support divisions, to advise HSC on its policy concerns, including legislation. They ensure, among other things, that HSC's proposals are legally sound, embody high technical and scientific standards, have taken into account EU and other international requirements and are, in practice, enforceable. Policy staff are active in consulting stakeholders, liasing with other Ministries, preparing briefing for Ministers and Parliament and in a wide variety of EU and international working groups concerned with new legislation and standards.

Inspection

24 . . . . . . Most of HSE's inspectors work, together with doctors and nurses of the Employment Medical Advisory Service (EMAS), in the Field Operations Directorate (FOD). The Directorate's offices are organised in regional groups across Britain; their work is mainly concerned with inspection and enforcement, but they have a variety of other responsibilities including local authority liaison, planning matters and giving medical advice. They also collect statistics and act as front-line contacts with the public who may, for example, seek advice on hazards affecting them.

25 . . . . . . Field Operations Directorate is organised on the basis of broad sector groupings, in which similar and synergistic industrial processes are brought together. In addition to the seven sectors and the railway industry, FOD has an Occupational Health and Environment Unit and a Safety Unit, which between them deal with health and safety issues across all sectors of employment. They also provide a source of expertise which supports the work of the 14 industry advisory and 7 Subject Advisory committees, and of directorates responsible for policy development.

26 . . . . . . The Nuclear Safety Directorate (NSD), is responsible for regulating nuclear safety. Under UK law nuclear plants in Great Britain cannot operate without a site licence issued by HSE. NSD sets out the conditions attached to a site licence, the general safety requirements to deal with the risks on a nuclear site and administers the licensing regime on behalf of HSE. The legal regime is complemented by the Ionising Radiations Regulations 1999 (IRR)[4] which provide for the protection of workers in all industries from ionising radiations, and by the generality of health and safety regulation, which NSD also enforces on nuclear sites.

27 . . . . . . The Hazardous Installations Directorate (HID) is responsible for enforcing health and safety legislation in 'upstream' petroleum and diving industries; sites where chemicals are manufactured or processed; large quantities of hazardous chemicals are stored, or where explosives are manufactured, processed or stored; pipelines transporting hazardous substances and road transport of hazardous substances, mining operations and mining exploratory drilling. HID also advises local authorities on planning for hazardous installations and other development in the vicinity of such installations.

▼ **Science and technology**

28 . . . . . . To enable HSE to be an effective regulator, and to ensure that the policy and standards it sets are technically sound and cost-effective, high quality scientific and technological underpinning is essential. HSE annually spends about £37 million on science and technology, around half on research and the other half on reactive work, including the investigation of incidents and the analysis and assembly of evidence to support enforcement action.

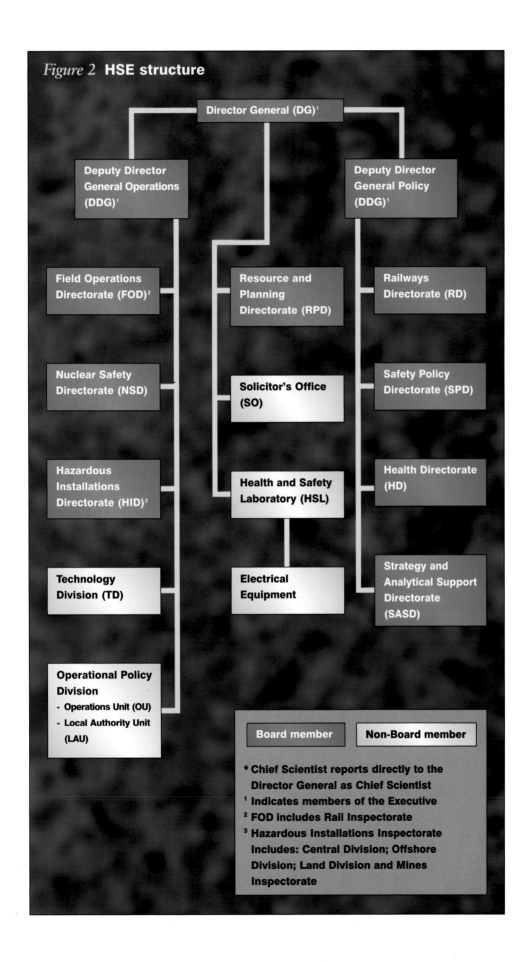

Figure 2 **HSE structure**

Director General (DG)[1]

Deputy Director General Operations (DDG)[1]

Deputy Director General Policy (DDG)[1]

Field Operations Directorate (FOD)[2]

Resource and Planning Directorate (RPD)

Railways Directorate (RD)

Nuclear Safety Directorate (NSD)

Solicitor's Office (SO)

Safety Policy Directorate (SPD)

Hazardous Installations Directorate (HID)[3]

Health and Safety Laboratory (HSL)

Health Directorate (HD)

Technology Division (TD)

Electrical Equipment

Strategy and Analytical Support Directorate (SASD)

Operational Policy Division
- **Operations Unit (OU)**
- **Local Authority Unit (LAU)**

Board member | **Non-Board member**

* **Chief Scientist reports directly to the Director General as Chief Scientist**
[1] **Indicates members of the Executive**
[2] **FOD includes Rail Inspectorate**
[3] **Hazardous Installations Inspectorate Includes: Central Division; Offshore Division; Land Division and Mines Inspectorate**

29 . . . . . . HSE's Science and Innovation Strategy describes how it applies science and technology in support of its mission to ensure that risks from work activities are properly controlled. In particular, the strategy explains how scientific resources are deployed to meet the business targets set out in the Strategic Plan.

30 . . . . . . Although most research is placed with external suppliers, HSE maintains an important in-house agency, the Health and Safety Laboratory (HSL). The primary role of HSL is to provide investigative work and other scientific services arising from HSE's day-to-day operation, which often requires a rapid multidisciplinary response. A large amount of the scientific and technological content of policy development operational casework is provided by staff who are highly qualified in a range of industrial and scientific disciplines, and work in Technology Division, Health Directorate, HSL, and the Operating Directorates. HSE's Chief Scientist is also the Director of HSE's Hazardous Installations Directorate. Many of these specialists are trained inspectors and contribute to, and sometimes lead, investigations of accidents and incidents. They also anticipate the health and safety consequences of science and technology trends, developing new approaches to the control of risks from work activities. They manage a national store of hazardous experience which is continuously clarified, updated and augmented as necessary.

Local authorities

31 . . . . . . Over 400 local authorities in England, Scotland and Wales, have responsibility for the enforcement of health and safety legislation in over 1 million premises. These include offices, shops, retail and wholesale distribution, hotel and catering establishments, petrol filling stations, residential care homes and the leisure industry.

32 . . . . . . More than 11 million people are employed at these premises which, by their nature, attract millions of members of the public through their doors every year.

33 . . . . . . In the retail, wholesale, hotel and catering, offices, residential care homes and the consumer/ leisure industries, local authorities will be the principal

enforcing authority. In each case, however, HSE may also have some enforcement responsibilities.

34 . . . . . . Inspectors in local authorities are typically Environmental Health Officers. Environmental Health Departments discharge their HSW Act enforcement duties alongside other local authority enforcement responsibilities, including food safety, pollution, housing etc.

The legal framework

▼ Duties imposed by the Act

35 . . . . . . The starting point and main principle of the HSW Act[1] is that it is those who create risk from work activity who are responsible for the protection of workers and the public from any consequences. The Act places specific responsibilities on employers, the self-employed, employees, designers, manufacturers, importers and suppliers. Associated legislation places additional duties on owners, licensees, managers and people in charge of premises. The main provisions of the Act express general duties, for example, upon employers to maintain a safe workplace, upon anyone who undertakes work activity to protect the public, and require that goods be designed so as to be safe and without risks to health. Employees are required to co-operate with their employers in taking care.

36 . . . . . . Some of the legal duties imposed by or under the Act are specific and mandatory, for example, a mine must always have two exits, or laboratories offering particular services must be approved by HSE. The duty to assess risks and take appropriate action is fundamental and absolute. Beyond that, many duties are expressed as goals or targets which are to be met 'so far as is reasonably practicable' or through exercising 'adequate control'. These qualifications imply some degree of latitude or judgement as to how far it is reasonable to go. To do something 'so far as is reasonably practicable', for example, means to ascertain and apply up-to-date good practice wherever it is established, since clearly it is always reasonably practicable to do that. Where good practice is not specified or obvious, it is reasonable to weigh the seriousness of the risk against the difficulty and cost of reducing or removing it. In such cases, risk-reducing measures must legally be pursued up to the point where the taking of any further steps would be grossly disproportionate to any residual risk. These rules are regardless of company size or economic circumstances.

37 . . . . . . In a very few cases the requirement of a regulation may be to do what is practicable or technically feasible. This means that whatever is specified must be done regardless of the expense.

▼   ## Regulations, codes of practice and guidance

38 . . . . . . The Act states that legislation passed before 1974 should be: 'progressively replaced by a system of regulations and approved codes of practice'. At the time the Act came into force there were some 30 statutes and 500 sets of regulations. In carrying out the reform of the law, the general principle has been that regulations, like the Act itself, should, so far as possible, express general duties, principles and goals and that subordinate detail should be set out in approved codes and guidance. Following the Review of Regulation in 1994 the process of reform continues. Further change results from the European legislative process, which sometimes imposes more detailed and specific requirements than would be envisaged under the Act.

39 . . . . . . Regulations are made by the appropriate Government Minister, normally on the basis of proposals submitted by the Commission after consultation, as previously explained. They have to be laid before Parliament, under which proposals automatically become law 21 days after being submitted to Parliament (unless objection is made).

40 . . . . . . Approved codes of practice (ACOPs) are approved by HSC with the consent of the appropriate Secretary of State; they do not require agreement from Parliament. ACOPs have a special authority in law. Failure to comply with the provisions may be taken by a court in criminal proceedings as evidence of a failure to comply with the requirements of the Act or of regulations to which the ACOP relates, unless it can be shown that those requirements were complied with in some equally effective way. Thus, ACOPs (which can be updated more easily) provide flexibility to cope with invention and technological change without a lowering of standards.

41 . . . . . . Other guidance is issued by the Commission or its advisory committees, or by HSE, in effect as a notification of the standards its inspectors will expect (following HSC/E guidance is not compulsory and employers are free to take other action). In addition, HSE issues a large volume of guidance adapted to the needs of local authority inspection. Each year HSC and HSE publish over 350 documents giving information, advice and guidance about different sectors or processes – at any one time there are approximately 1200 priced titles and 800 free titles in print.

Other legislation

42   Some legislation existing prior to the 1974 Act remains in force, including legislation covering mines, railways and nuclear safety, some parts of the Factories Act 1961 and the Offices, Shops and Railway Premises Act 1963.[5,6]

43   Under the Nuclear Installations Act 1965,[7] the Executive is the licensing authority for nuclear installations and it supervises mining qualifications under the Management and Administration of Safety and Health at Mines Regulations 1993.[8] The Railway Inspectorate approves new railway works and changes to existing works, by means of regulations made under the Transport and Works Act 1992.[9]

European legislation

44   In recent years, most legislation on health and safety has been introduced to implement European Directives – mainly directly promoting minimum standards for the health and safety of workers but also via measures designed to complete and maintain the single market or protect the environment. There is now a developed body of EU health and safety law. A key element is the Framework Directive (implemented in 1993 by the Management Regulations), which established broadly based obligations for employers to evaluate, avoid and reduce workplace risks etc. A range of related and other directives (implemented via national regulations) cover the use of work equipment, manual handling, health, safety and welfare in the workplace, personal protective equipment, carcinogens at work, display screen equipment, construction, safety signs, pregnant women, noise, asbestos, chemical and biological agents, explosive atmospheres etc. A range of single market and environmental measures cover chemicals, dangerous substances and preparations, genetically manipulated organisms and major hazards etc.

Standards

45   Most health and safety standards derive originally from the practice of inspection. The need to give advice or apply the law consistently gives rise to a process of standardisation of practice, which is incorporated into the advice which inspectors give. Hence inspection standards evolve. Such

internal inspection standards, once established, are likely to be published as informal guidance, be taken into account by advisory committees preparing more formal guidance, and by the Executive in developing new regulations and codes. They may also be used in participating in the development of formal standards documents through national and international institutions.

46 . . . . . . The British Standards Institution (BSI) is the national body responsible for the development of British Standards. The vast majority of these are transposed European or international standards. BSI's is the gateway to UK participation in Comité Europeen de Normalisation (CEN) and International Organization for Standardization (ISO) and, through the British Electrotechnical Committees, in Comité Europeen de Normalisation Electrotechnique (CENELEC) and International Electrotechnique Commission (IEC). HSE is a major contributor – often on behalf of BSI – to the development of many of the standards which have health and/or safety aspects. Standards vary in type from specifications of performance goals, to guidance on operational practice, to design criteria for industrial products. They are sometimes referred to in HSE's published guidance and occasionally, use of standards is required in health and safety regulations and codes. In a policy statement published in 1996, the HSC emphasised the continuing importance of standards as a form of guidance in promoting health and safety. The statement also said that HSE would make a major contribution to standard making where health and safety matters appear to justify it and resources are available.

47 . . . . . . The development of harmonised safety standards in support of 'New Approach' directives made under Article 95 (formerly Article 100a) of the Treaty of Rome has represented a substantial element of HSE's work in connection with the single market. These standards are of particular importance since they allow manufacturers to design and build products to the harmonised standards, and then claim they have met the essential health and safety requirements in the relevant directives.

The policy process

48 . . . . . . In developing its policy, HSE follows the principles of good regulation as adopted by the UK Government under the following headings:

▼ **transparent** – legislation must be clear and easy to understand with aims written in clear and simple language, people and businesses are given an opportunity to comment and time to comply before introduction;

▼ **accountable** – HSE/HSC answers to Ministers, parliament and the public for any legislation it proposes, with appeals procedures for enforcement actions

▼ **targeted** – legislation is focused on the problems and reduces adverse side effects to a minimum, where possible being goal-based, and regularly reviewed for effectiveness;

▼ **consistent** – new legislation is consistent with existing regulations – in health and safety and other subjects, and compatible with international law and standards;

▼ **proportionate** – the effect which regulations have on people and businesses provide a balance between risk and cost, and alternatives to state regulation are fully considered.

49 . . . . . . To follow these principles, policy staff are responsible for considering a wide range of options during the development of any legislative initiative, whether this originates from the identification of an issue peculiar to Great Britain or from a European or international initiative. This starts with the collection of evidence to justify the intervention – from various sources, such as experience with enforcement of existing legislation, scientific data and, if necessary, specially commissioned research. Alternative solutions, including non-legislative ones, are considered, their impacts assessed, and associated existing legislation considered for contradictions or compatibility. We are particularly concerned to ensure that our proposals do not discriminate unfairly against any person or group.

50 . . . . . . Once the alternative solutions have been developed, this analysis is made available to a wide range of interest groups and the public for their views. These consultations frequently take place in two stages – the issue of a Discussion Document, where the problem is described and views are sought on appropriate action – and a Consultative Document, where the details of

the options are presented and views sought on practicability. The results of this policy development process and the consultations are then presented to HSC for them to advise Ministers on the appropriateness of the regulations, if this is the option selected. If all agree that regulation is necessary, associated guidance is produced and issued well in advance of the implementation date of the regulations. This process is designed to obtain broad public support, avoid unintentional consequences, produce a solution which is enforceable, and balances the risks, costs and benefits.

Regulatory impact assessment

51   All proposals for legislation and published guidance with the force of law which have an impact on businesses, charities or the voluntary sector need to be supported by a regulatory impact assessment (RIA). This:

▼ identifies the problems and the specific objectives of the proposals;

▼ assesses the risks;

▼ compares the benefits and costs of a range of options, including a 'do nothing' case, and non-regulatory solutions;

▼ summarises who or what sectors bear these costs and benefits, and identifies any issues of equity or fairness;

▼ outlines the impact on small firms and any measures to help them comply;

▼ sets out the arrangements for securing compliance, with details of sanctions for non-compliance;

▼ identifies how the policy will be monitored and evaluated, with results feeding back into the process of policy development.

The impact assessment develops throughout the policy process, a draft accompanies the consultative document and feedback is used to refine the analysis. The final results are presented to Ministers, who having read the RIA sign a statement, which states they are satisfied that '…the benefits justify the costs'.

Evaluation and review

52   Plans for evaluation of the impact of the legislation are required before their introduction. These use the data gathered earlier in the process, which was used to justify the intervention, to contribute to a definition of a baseline

and to allow the impact of the regulations to be quantified. The success of the legislation will be judged against how well it meets its objectives. Legislation, once introduced, is normally evaluated against a pre-announced timetable. The aim is to repeat this process at intervals to identify whether the legislation should be modified or repealed. This avoids having a growing raft of archaic legislation – which could potentially be a problem due to Britain's long, unbroken, legislative history.

Enforcement

▼ ## Powers of inspectors

53 . . . . . . The main object of inspection is to stimulate compliance with health and safety legislation and to ensure that a good standard of protection is maintained. Inspectors have, and make use of, important statutory powers. They can enter any premises where work is carried on, without giving notice. They can talk to employees and safety representatives, take photographs and samples, and impound dangerous equipment and substances. If they are not satisfied by the levels of health and safety standards being achieved, they have several means of obtaining improvements:

▼ advice or warnings;

▼ improvement or prohibition notices. An improvement notice requires a contravention to be remedied in a specified time. A prohibition notice, issued if there is, or is likely to be, a risk of serious personal injury, requires an activity to be stopped immediately or after a specified time, unless remedial action is taken. There is a right of appeal to tribunals; the improvement notice is suspended but a prohibition notice remains in force until the appeal is held, unless the employment tribunal directs otherwise;

▼ prosecution in the criminal law courts. In England and Wales, most cases are heard by magistrates who may, for serious offences, impose a maximum fine of £20 000. The magistrates refer some cases to Crown Courts where there is no limit on the fine which may be imposed. In Scotland, most cases are taken in the sheriff courts either on summary procedure or an indictment procedure before a jury. Certain very serious offences, for example, that of failing to comply with a prohibition notice, may attract a prison sentence. A prosecution may be mounted against either individuals or corporate bodies, including nationalised industries or local authorities;

▼ in the case of a death resulting from a work activity the possibility that manslaughter might be involved is always considered. Manslaughter investigations are a police responsibility.

▼ informal investigation of particular accidents or incidents, so as to learn lessons or prepare legal action. There are various means of disseminating the experience gained in such investigations, for example, by publishing studies and reports.

54 . . . . . . Each year some 2500 charges are laid against employers by HSE and local authority inspectors (by the Crown Office and procurator fiscal service in Scotland). The number of notices issued by inspectors in 1999/2000 was approximately 17 400. About 85% of information laid results in a conviction. Inspectors decide what enforcement action is appropriate in accordance with HSC's published enforcement policy statement. HSC policy requires that enforcement action should be proportionate to the risk created; targeted on the most serious risks, or where hazards are least well controlled, consistent and transparent.

55 . . . . . . HSC is empowered to direct that formal inquiries should be conducted and reports published. It may do this by setting up an inquiry, or by directing HSE to carry out a technical inquiry. In all such cases the reports are published.

▼ **The planning of inspections**

56 . . . . . . HSE's inspection visits may take place in response to a complaint from a worker or an inquiry by a member of the public, or to follow up previous inquiries or to conduct investigations. But the majority, largely made without warning, are planned as part of a major programme of preventive inspection designed to check on standards, gather information and secure compliance with the law, both at fixed establishments and temporary worksites such as construction sites. Inspectors may also visit the head offices of major national companies to discuss and secure improvements in the management of safety throughout the company.

57 . . . . . . To an increasing extent, each HSE regional office develops and manages its own inspection programme according to local need, but it does so within a national planning system that focuses inspection towards workplaces and processes which present the highest risks. In prioritising the work in this way, extensive use is made of computer systems. Databases record information on employers and workplaces, obtained from previous contacts and inspections, and provide details about numbers of employees at risk, hazardous processes, hazardous substances, accident history etc. Each workplace is rated taking account of:

▼ hazards;

▼ levels of risk to the health and safety of employees;

▼ levels of risk to the health and safety of the public;

▼ working conditions;

▼ management attitudes and abilities;

▼ the accident rate in the relevant employment sector.

58 . . . . . . Data from computer systems is also used to influence individual employers to set priorities for action within their own organisations. HSE's FOCUS computer system enables the aggregation of data on major firms to help review the health and safety aspects of their central management systems.

59 . . . . . . Local authorities are also guided in their inspections and investigations by the HSC's priorities, through the HELA Strategic Plan.

▼ A systems approach

60 . . . . . . Assessment of the quality of health and safety management is a very important element in HSE's approach to inspection. Companies are obliged by law to set out their health and safety policies and are increasingly encouraged to define and monitor their management systems. HSE's inspectors are trained in how to assess management systems, and are able to carry out audits. HSE learns about beneficial developments in health and safety management, such as the relevance of the principles of quality management techniques, and provides guidance on their use.

▼ Training inspectors

61 . . . . . . HSE places great emphasis on recruitment and training of all its staff, relying as it does on a very wide range of professional skills. Almost all HSE inspectors are graduates who following recruitment undertake a two-year professional training course. A programme of field training under the supervision of experienced inspectors is integrated with a specially designed academic course, which leads to the award of a post-graduate diploma in occupational health and safety. All HSE inspectors share access to programmes of mid-career training which keep them professionally well equipped and in tune with the latest thinking in other directorates of HSE and outside. Guidance is also issued to local authorities on the training and competence of local authority enforcement officers.

▼ **Sharing experience**

62 . . . . . . Operational Policy Division, which reports to the Deputy Director General Operations, encourages the sharing of best regulatory practice such as models of enforcement management, develops and produces corporate operational policies and procedures, provides a focus for inspection excellence, enables issues of common concern to all enforcing authorities to be identified and discussed and, through local authorities, ensures that HSC's objectives are achieved in the local authority enforced sector.

▼ **Local authorities**

63 . . . . . . HELA was set up in 1975 to provide effective liaison between HSE and local authorities. It seeks to ensure that health and safety legislation is enforced in a consistent way among local authorities, and between local authorities and HSE. HELA provides a national forum for discussion and exchange of information on enforcement of legislation. It promotes the achievement of good health and safety standards and practices. HELA reports annually to HSC on behalf of local authorities.

▼ **Charging schemes**

64 . . . . . . In accordance with Government policy, the HSC charges duty holders who operate 'permissioning regimes' requiring regulatory approval for certain activities, eg testing, licensing, certification, approvals, exemption and acceptance of notifications. The HSC charging policy applies to the major hazards industries – gas transportation, offshore and onshore petrochemicals, and the railway industry.

65 . . . . . . Charges are made for inspection, investigations, the assessment of safety cases or reports, and in the railway industry only, for approval of new or modified works, plant and equipment.

66 . . . . . . Tripartite Charging Review Groups for each of the industry sectors oversee the effectiveness and efficiency of the charging schemes.

Control of risks at the workplace

Risk assessment

67 . . . . . . Risk assessment underpins HSC/E's approach to the regulation of risk from work activities. The approach is described in the publication, *Reducing risks, protecting people*,[11] which sets out the factors that inform regulatory decisions, for example, scientific knowledge, the practicability of control measures and public attitudes to the risks and benefits. If the combination of individual risk and societal concerns is so great that it cannot be reduced to a tolerable level, the activity, process or substance will need to be banned. However, HSC starts from the position that the risks from hazardous activities at work can be adequately controlled, different measures and techniques being appropriate in different situations.

68 . . . . . . Risk assessment also ensures that the employer's response in managing risk is commensurate with the risk. The principle of risk assessment is implicit in the HSW Act. It is also explicit in the Management of Health and Safety at Work Regulations which (together with existing legislation) implemented the Framework Directive (89/391/EEC). HSE has issued a guidance leaflet, *Five steps to risk assessment*,[12] to help employers and the self-employed assess risks and meet their legal obligations. The five steps are:

▼ look for the hazard;

▼ decide who might be harmed and how;

▼ evaluate the risk arising from the hazard and decide whether existing precautions are adequate or more should be done;

▼ record the findings (if there are five or more employees);

▼ review the assessment and revise it if necessary.

69 . . . . . . Essential elements of the British approach to health and safety management and the control of risk are set out below.

Health and safety policies

70 . . . . . . Employers with five or more employees are required to prepare a written statement of their general health and safety policy, setting out aims and

objectives for improving health and safety and the arrangements they have in force for achieving their objectives. This must be brought to the attention of employees.

Consultation

71 . . . . . . In workplaces where trade unions are recognised, the unions have the right to appoint safety representatives to act on the employees' behalf in consultations with their employer about health and safety matters. Employers must consult with any employees not represented by an appointed safety representative, either directly or through representatives elected by the employees concerned.

Health and safety assistance

72 . . . . . . Employers must appoint one or more competent persons to provide occupational health and safety assistance. Competent persons should be appointed from amongst the workforce, or where they do not exist, from external services. In particular employers may need competent help in devising and applying measures to protect workers' health and safety. They may also need the help from other experts such as health professionals to advise them of the effects of work on health and vice-versa, health surveillance as indicated by the risk assessment of fitness for work and rehabilitating workers back into work. All workers are covered by the National Health Service through family doctors who have access to HSE's Employment Medical Advisory Service (EMAS) for advice on their patients' occupational health problems.

Licensing

73 . . . . . . Licensing or approval regimes are reserved for areas where the nature of the roles or other potential effects demand detailed controls. Under such a regime, HSE's Nuclear Safety Directorate ensures that nuclear installations are designed, constructed, commissioned, operated, maintained and decommissioned to the highest standards of safety. Other hazards covered by licensing include the manufacture and storage of explosives and work with asbestos.

▼ Safety reports and safety cases

74 . . . . . . Safety reports for major hazard installations identify and evaluate the hazards and describe the management system and the precautions designed to prevent, control or minimise the consequences of any significant accident. HSE does not formally accept the safety reports. Licensing decisions for nuclear installations are based primarily on an assessment of a safety case. The safety requirements for offshore installations are similar to those described above. However an installation is not allowed to operate unless it has a current safety case which has been accepted by HSE. Offshore safety cases have to include provision for internal audit to ensure that the arrangements are kept under regular review. The outputs from safety cases and safety report assessments are used by inspectors to determine inspection priorities, and as a standard against which to judge the operator's performance during subsequent inspections. A similar safety case regime has operated on the railways since 1994. All infrastructure controllers, train and station operators are required to have an accepted safety case.

Insurance and compensation

75 . . . . . . Employees who are injured or made ill at work are entitled to sue their employer for compensation in the civil courts – in order to succeed they need to establish that their employer was negligent, or in breach of statutory duty (or both). All employers are required by law to take out compulsory insurance against their civil liabilities. This does not give the employee automatic right to compensation, but if the employee's civil action succeeds, the insurance will ensure that the employer can pay the compensation that is due. The insurance policy must provide cover of at least £5 million rising out of any one occurrence.

76 . . . . . . The insurance is provided by private insurance companies, who also provide some preventive services, particularly in testing high-risk plant. These services may take the form of advice offered on a commercial basis or as part of the insurance package they negotiate with particular operators. Some, however, are carried out on a statutory basis; thus for example, insurers may carry out statutory inspection of safety-critical plant such as pressure vessels and lifting machinery, as required by law.

77 . . . . . . Any employee who is injured or made ill at work is also entitled to claim benefits under the state social security system as well as receiving treatment from the National Health Service. The Industrial Injuries Scheme provides preferential Social Security benefits for disablements caused by an accident or a prescribed occupational disease arising out of or in the course of employment. It is not necessary to have paid National Insurance contributions to be eligible for these benefits. Benefit is paid irrespective of fault on the part of the employer; it can be paid even though the employee was at fault.

Table 1 **Numbers of HSE staff, April 2001**	
Solicitor's Office	22
Resources and Planning Directorate	500
Health Directorate	245
Safety Policy Directorate	127
Strategy and Analytical Support Directorate	103
Operations Group	
Operations Unit	13
Local Authority Unit	17
Field Operations Directorate & HM Railway Inspectorate	1567
Hazardous Installations Directorate	526
Nuclear Safety Directorate	247
Electrical Equipment Certification Service	44
Technology Division	123
Total HSE staff	**3534**
Health and Safety Laboratory	360
Total Staff	**3894**

Local authorities

78 In 1999/2000 some 3 650 local authority officers enforced health and safety legislation. This was equivalent to 1 110 full-time officers.

References

1 . . . . . . *Health and Safety at Work etc Act 1974* SI 1974/1439
The Stationery Office 1974 **ISBN 0 11 141439 X**

2 . . . . . . *Management of Health and Safety at Work Regulations (MHSWR)1999*
SI 1999/3242 The Stationery Office 2000 **ISBN 0 11 0856252 2**

3 . . . . . . *Health and Safety (Enforcing Authority) Regulations 1998* SI 1998/494
The Stationery Office 1998 **ISBN 0 11 065642 3**

4 . . . . . . *Ionising Radiations Regulations 1999 (IRRs)* SI 1999/3232
The Stationery Office 1999 **ISBN 0 11 085614 7**

5 . . . . . . *Factories Act 1961* The Stationery Office 1961 **ISBN 0 10 850027 6**

6 . . . . . . *Offices, Shops and Railways Premises Act 1963 Ch 42*
The Stationery Office 1963 **ISBN 0 10 850111 6**

7 . . . . . . *Nuclear Installations Act 1965* The Stationery Office 1965
ISBN 0 10 850216 3

8 . . . . . . *The Management and Administration of Safety and Health at Mines*
Regulations 1993 SI 1993/1897 The Stationery Office 1993
ISBN 0 11 034897 4

9 . . . . . . *Transport and Works Act 1992* SI 1992/1347 The Stationery Office 1992
ISBN 0 11 024347 1

10 . . . . . . *HELA 2001 Report on Health and Safety in the Local Authority Enforced*
Sectors Health and Safety Commission 2001

11 . . . . . . *Reducing risks, protecting people* HSE Books 2001 **ISBN 0 7176 2151 0**

12 . . . . . . *Five steps to risk assessment* Leaflet INDG163(rev1) HSE Books 1998
(single copy free or priced packs of 10 **ISBN 0 7176 1565 0**)

While every effort has been made to ensure the accuracy of the references listed in this publication, their future availability cannot be guaranteed.

Further information

The Health and Safety Commission and Executive publish a wide range of guidance on health and safety issues. A sample of the publications and databases available is given here.

Publications

General

Health and Safety Commission Annual Report and *The Health and Safety Commission/Executive Accounts 2000/01*   HSE Books 2001
  ISBN 0 10 291307 2

Health and safety statistics 2000/01   HSE Books 2001   **ISBN 0 7176 2110 3**

Health and Safety Commission Strategic Plan 2001/2004 Misc 319
  HSE Books 2001

Guidance

A guide to the Health and Safety at Work etc Act 1974 L1
  HSE Books 1990   **ISBN 0 7176 0441 1**

Essentials of health and safety at work (Third edition)   HSE Books 2000
  ISBN 0 7176 0716 X

Health surveillance at work HSG61 (Second edition)   HSE Books 1999
  ISBN 0 7176 1705 X

Successful health and safety management HSG65 (Second edition)
  HSE Books 1997   **ISBN 0 7176 1276 7**

Occupational exposure limits 2001 EH40/2001 (updated annually)
  HSE Books 2001   **ISBN 0 7176 1977 X**

The cost to Britain of workplace accidents and work-related ill health in 1995/96
  HSG101 (Second edition)   HSE Books 1999   **ISBN 0 7176 1709 2**

HSE priced and free publications are available by mail order from HSE Books, PO Box 1999, Sudbury, Suffolk CO10 2WA Tel: 01787 881165 Fax: 01787 313995 Website: www.hsebooks.co.uk (HSE priced publications are also available from bookshops.)

Subscription services available from HSE

Health and Safety Commission Newsletter

Issued six times a year, this publication provides up-to-date information on UK and European health and safety issues. Each issue takes an in-depth look at real incidents and accidents, the European scene and how it affects UK business, legislation and new codes of practice and guidance on a wide range of industrial processes and hazards.

HSE News Bulletin

This is a weekly compilation of all press releases issued by HSE's press office on a variety of subjects relating to health and safety in the workplace.

Toxic Substances Bulletin (TSB)

This is available on HSE's website at: www.hse.gov.uk/toxicsubstances/ Issues will be available for free viewing and downloading for personal use in May, September and January. Pre-printed versions will be available from HSE Books for £3 per copy.

New Books News

This free ad hoc newsletter provides details of new HSC/E publications as well as information relating to relevant parliamentary publications such as Regulations. In addition, HSE Books issues a catalogue every six months listing publications, electronic products and videos which can be ordered.

General HSE enquiries

For information about health and safety ring HSE's InfoLine Tel: 08701 545500 Fax: 02920 859260 e-mail: hseinformationservices@natbrit.com or write to HSE Information Services, Caerphilly Business Park, Caerphilly CF83 3GG. You can also visit HSE's website: www.hse.gov.uk

Hsedirect

Available via the Internet, www.hsedirect.com, or alternatively on CD-Rom, hsedirect provides access to:

▼ all the latest health and safety legislation;

▼ ACOPs and HSE guidance on legislation, including the L, COP and HSR series;

▼ HSE guidance on workplaces, processes and substances, including the HSG series and priced Industry Advisory Committee publications;

▼ a selection of the most commonly used HSE forms.

The service also contains HSE press releases, consultative documents, an events diary and links to relevant sites. There are a variety of subscription options. For further information, visit www.hsedirect.com, or call hsedirect enquires on 0845 3003142.

Translations

Translations commissioned by HSE staff are subsequently made available for sale to the public and are listed in a half-yearly Translations Bulletin published on the HSE website.

For further information contact: HSE Language Service, Broad Lane, Sheffield S3 7HQ   Tel: 0114 289 2339   Fax: 0114 289 2333

Printed and published by the Health and Safety Executive   C20   03/02